Americana

MUSCLE CARS THEN AND NOW

Abdo & Daughters
MIDDLE GRADE NONFICTION
An Imprint of Abdo Publishing
abdobooks.com

R.L. Van

ABDOBOOKS.COM

Published by Abdo Publishing, a division of ABDO, PO Box 398166, Minneapolis, Minnesota 55439.

Printed in the United States of America, North Mankato, Minnesota

102023

012024

THIS BOOK CONTAINS RECYCLED MATERIALS

Design: Kelly Doudna, Mighty Media, Inc.

Production: Denise Hamernik, Mighty Media, Inc.

Editor: Liz Salzmann

Cover Photographs: Getty Images (both)

Interior Photographs: AP Images, p. 40; Flickr, pp. 6-7, 20, 37, 38-39; Getty Images, p. 1 (both); Library of Congress, p. 21; Mighty Media, Inc., pp. 42-43; Shutterstock Images, pp. 3, 4-5, 8-9, 10-11, 12-13, 14-15, 18-19, 23, 24-25, 26, 27, 28-29, 30, 32, 33, 34, 44, 45; Wikimedia Commons, pp. 16-17, 22

Design Elements: iStockphoto

LIBRARY OF CONGRESS CONTROL NUMBER: 2023939344

PUBLISHER'S CATALOGING-IN-PUBLICATION DATA

Names: Van, R.L., author.

Title: Muscle cars: then and now / by R.L. Van

Other title: then and now

Description: Minneapolis, Minnesota : Abdo Publishing, 2024 | Series: Americana | Includes online resources and index.

Identifiers: ISBN 9781098291761 (lib. bdg.) | ISBN 9781098278663 (ebook)

Subjects: LCSH: Americana--Juvenile literature. | Muscle cars--Juvenile literature. | Hot rods--Juvenile literature. | History, Modern--Juvenile literature.

Classification: DDC 973.0--dc23

TABLE OF CONTENTS

Alabama International Motor Speedway was renamed Talladega Superspeedway in 1989.

Chapter 1

NEED FOR SPEED

It's March 24, 1970. Star race car driver Buddy Baker climbs into the Dodge Charger Daytona. He is at Alabama International Motor Speedway in Talladega, Alabama. Baker and his team plan to test the car's transmission. But Baker also has another goal. No one in the National Association for Stock Car Auto Racing (NASCAR) has ever officially driven faster than 200 miles per hour (322 kmh) on a closed course. Today, Baker hopes to do just that.

Baker's crew adjusts the car's chassis. They make sure it's perfectly flat. There's no lift in the front, and the wing creates downforce on the back. This helps the car turn corners on the track. Baker drives lap after lap. The Daytona approaches the goal: 194 . . . 198.5 . . . 199.8 . . . NASCAR's chief timer and scorer lets out a cheer. Baker's last lap speed was more than 200 miles per hour. The Dodge Charger Daytona is the first car to exceed 200 miles per hour on a closed course! Baker's crew celebrates. Together, he, his team, and their muscle car just made NASCAR history.

Muscle Cars Then and Now

Muscle cars aren't only driven by professional race car drivers. In fact, these cars have been driven by everyday Americans for decades. They are more than just a means of transportation. For many Americans, muscle cars are symbols of style, rebellion, freedom, and even America itself.

Since the first muscle cars were released beginning in 1949, they have been an important part of American life and culture. These cars

have both influenced and been influenced by American culture. Today, muscle cars continue to impact Americans, whether as the latest models or as refurbished originals. As manufacturers innovate, it's likely that muscle cars will continue to inspire excitement and nostalgia in car lovers in the United States and around the world for years to come.

Buddy Baker drove a Ranier Racing No. 28 Oldsmobile, nicknamed "the Gray Ghost," in the 1980 Daytona 500. As of 2023, the car holds the fastest Daytona 500 run at 177.6 miles per hour (285.8 kmh).

The marketing team at Pontiac coined the term *muscle car* in 1964 when they used it to describe the new GTO.

Chapter 2

BUILDING MUSCLE

Which cars can be considered muscle cars is often debated by car enthusiasts. But most people agree on a basic definition. Muscle cars are usually affordable midsize American cars with powerful V-8 engines. They're typically two-door cars with rear-wheel drive. Many of them are high-performance versions of standard cars. The concept of muscle cars evolved over time. In fact, the first muscle cars weren't called "muscle cars" at all. The development of muscle cars and their role in American culture took place throughout the mid-1900s.

The Dawn of the Muscle Car

Long before car manufacturers began producing muscle cars, Americans were building hot rods. Hot-rodders updated old cars to make them powerful drag racing machines. This practice became especially popular in the years following World War II. Meanwhile, NASCAR was conceived in 1947 and began holding stock car races the next year. Both hot rods and stock cars were ordinary cars with racing modifications. *Hot Rod* magazine began publication in 1948 as well, increasing public interest in these cars even more.

With Americans' growing enthusiasm for these powered-up vehicles, General Motors (GM) released the 1949 Oldsmobile Rocket 88. Though opinions vary, many consider it to be the first muscle car. The car had a uniquely powerful engine in a lightweight Oldsmobile body. The Rocket 88 quickly captured public attention and admiration. It dominated in stock car racing. Other manufacturers rushed to put out similar high-performance cars. The Rocket 88 is often credited with starting the muscle car craze in the United States. It even inspired the song "Rocket 88," which many consider the first rock 'n' roll song ever recorded.

Throughout the 1950s and early 1960s, many car manufacturers built full-size high-performance vehicles. They also offered buyers special upgrades for increased speed and power. Race car drivers used these performance models in races, helping companies build strong public images. Compact cars were introduced in 1960, and midsize cars soon followed. In 1962, Dodge and Plymouth created midsize performance cars that dominated at the racetrack and drew even greater public attention.

In 1949, race car driver Red Byron won the NASCAR series Strictly Stock division in a Rocket 88.

The Pontiac GTO

In the early 1960s, GM had a rule that its midsize cars couldn't have engines over a certain size. Engineer John DeLorean worked for Pontiac, which was part of GM. He wanted to build a performance car that would appeal to younger buyers. He and his team replaced the engine in the midsize Tempest with a larger one to create the GTO. To get around GM's rule, they made the larger engine an option rather than part of the standard model.

The 1969 GTO was nicknamed "the Judge" because of a popular skit called "Here Comes the Judge" from the comedy TV show *Rowan & Martin's Laugh-In.*

The 1964 Pontiac GTO was a huge success. Pontiac had expected to sell 5,000 in its first year, but it sold 32,000. An advertising executive at GM, Jim Wangers, drew people in with marketing that highlighted the GTO's power, speed, and acceleration.

Many people believe that the GTO was the first true muscle car. But regardless of whether the performance cars that came before it were true muscle cars, the GTO kicked off what is now considered the Muscle Car Era or the Golden Age of Muscle Cars.

An Exciting Era

Through the 1960s and into the early 1970s, other American car manufacturers released their own midsize muscle cars. Competition between companies led to stylish new models that outdid each other in performance year after year. Manufacturers also started making smaller cars with V-8 engines, such as the Ford Mustang. These smaller performance vehicles eventually became known as pony cars. Some muscle car enthusiasts don't consider them muscle cars at all. Others believe that pony cars are muscle cars if they include the best possible performance engines and other options.

Muscle cars continued to increase in popularity. They generally cost less than other types of cars available at the time. This made them more accessible to young people. During this time, nearly every American car manufacturer was producing muscle cars. It was considered the norm for Americans to have them.

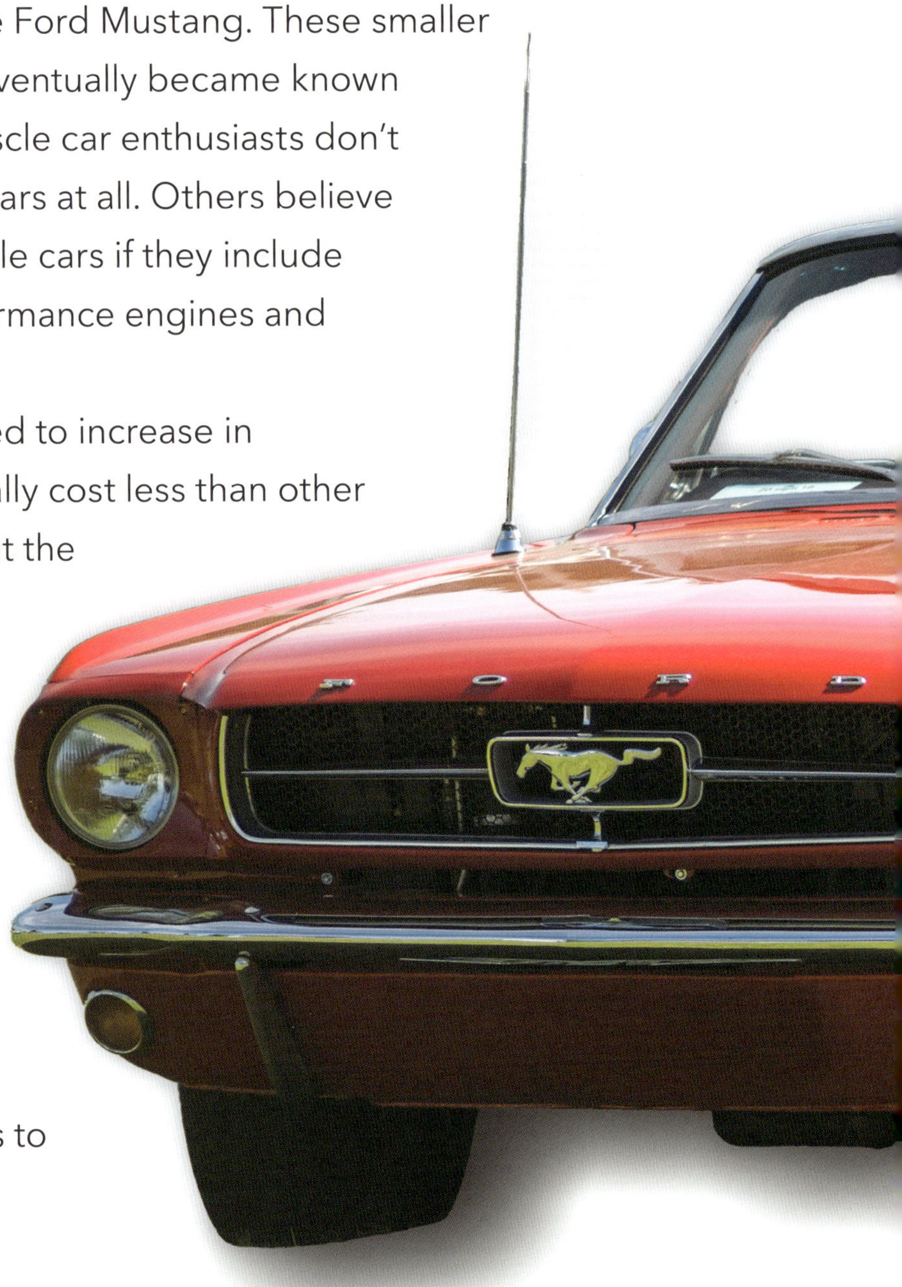

Cool Culture

Muscle cars and American culture have been intertwined since before the first muscle car was built. Hot rods, the precursor to muscle cars, were associated with illegal street racing. Hot rods themselves had origins in outrunning police during Prohibition. But muscle cars made this outlaw hot rod culture mainstream.

The Ford Mustang debuted at the New York World's Fair in April 1964.

Muscle cars and the cars they were based on were enormously successful thanks to American culture in the 1960s. It was a time when many young people valued nonconformity and rebellion. Manufacturers designed and advertised cars with the youth culture in mind. They produced muscle cars in bright colors and gave them hip performance package names. Cars had fun logos and mascots. For example, Plymouth partnered with film company Warner Brothers to release a model called the Plymouth Road Runner. It featured the Road Runner cartoon character and a cartoonish-sounding horn.

The Plymouth Road Runner Superbird was a version of the Dodge Daytona.

Muscle cars influenced American culture as much as American culture influenced the cars. Hollywood movies revolved around muscle cars. Hit songs about cars played on the radio. Young people broke the law to race their muscle cars in the streets. Drivers chose cars such as the GTO, with its rule-breaking engine, to build up their own rebellious images.

Muscle car drivers sometimes spin their tires before accelerating. This is known as burning rubber and is another cause of air pollution.

Chapter 3

DECLINE AND REVIVAL

In the 1970s, US cars as a whole, and especially muscle cars, struggled. A number of changes in the United States and around the world led to the decline of muscle cars' popularity. The years from 1973 to 1983 in the US car market are called the Malaise Era. It had lasting effects on American car culture and on muscle car production. But while muscle cars never returned to the glory days of the Muscle Car Era, they did eventually begin revving and racing again.

Hard Times

The powerful engines that gave muscle cars their appeal contributed to the cars' decline. In 1970, the US Congress passed the Clean Air Act. It required car manufacturers to make adjustments to engines in order to reduce carbon dioxide emissions. These engine adjustments led to less powerful vehicles. Additionally, new safety regulations meant manufacturers had to add

RALPH NADER

In 1965, consumer and environmental activist Ralph Nader wrote the book *Unsafe at Any Speed*. It revealed significant safety issues with American cars. This contributed to higher insurance rates for more dangerous cars, such as muscle cars. The book showed that many American performance cars, including muscle cars, weren't built to handle the high horsepower the engines generated. The findings in the book led to the first major US automobile safety laws. These were outlined in the 1966 National Traffic and Motor Vehicle Safety Act and the Highway Safety Act.

features such as larger bumpers, which added weight, making cars slower.

In 1973 and 1974, the Organization of Petroleum Exporting Countries (OPEC) reduced oil exports to the United States. This led to gas shortages and rising gas prices. Another gas crisis followed in 1979. Because muscle cars required a lot of gas, consumers' interest in them dropped. Car insurance rates also rose for muscle car owners. The cars were more dangerous and had higher crash rates than other types of vehicles. The cost of owning a muscle car led many consumers to look elsewhere.

Manufacturers stopped producing many models of muscle cars. The ones they continued producing were much less powerful. Some manufacturers focused on turning their performance cars into expensive luxury vehicles. Others simply tried to make their cars look like flashy muscle cars, but without the powerful, high-performance engines.

The Malaise Era was a time in American automobile history, but it echoed American culture. The high gas prices and economic crisis made Americans anxious. In 1979, US President Jimmy Carter gave a speech that came to be known as "the malaise speech." He shared his fears that Americans were using material goods to try to deal with feelings of emptiness. He said that Americans had lost confidence in the country. Carter noted that for the first time in American history, most people felt the economy would be worse over the next five years than it had been during the previous five.

The gas shortages in the 1970s led to long lines of cars at gas stations.

Looking Up

Though things looked bleak, there was still hope for muscle cars during this time. Despite the changes Pontiac was forced to make, sales of its Firebird pony cars improved even during the gas crisis in 1973 and 1974. This proved that people still wanted high-performance cars. Some pony cars from the late 1970s also demonstrated that it was possible to balance high power with new regulations.

Then, after the struggles of the Malaise Era, the 1980s brought a rebirth of muscle cars. Gas became available and affordable again, increasing drivers' interest in performance vehicles. Additionally, though imported cars were increasingly popular, buyers were still drawn to the all-American image of muscle cars.

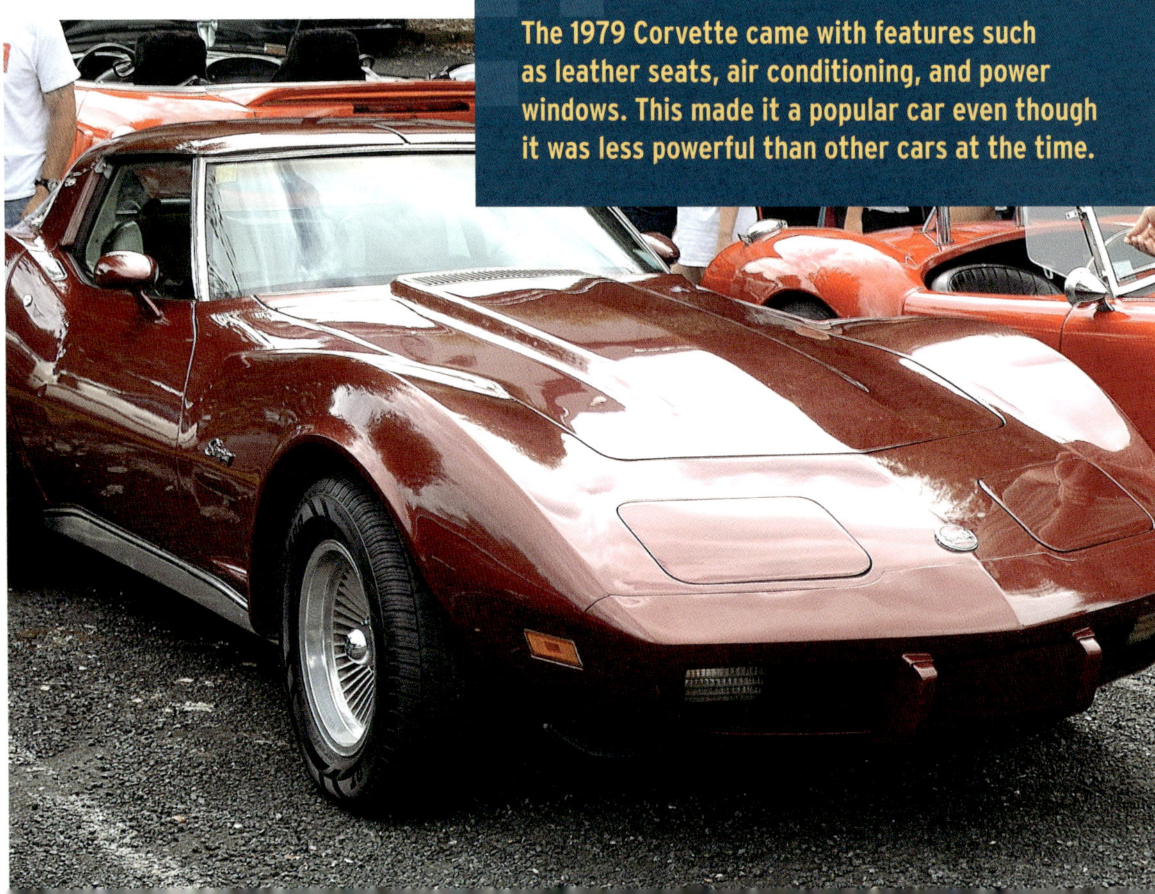

The 1979 Corvette came with features such as leather seats, air conditioning, and power windows. This made it a popular car even though it was less powerful than other cars at the time.

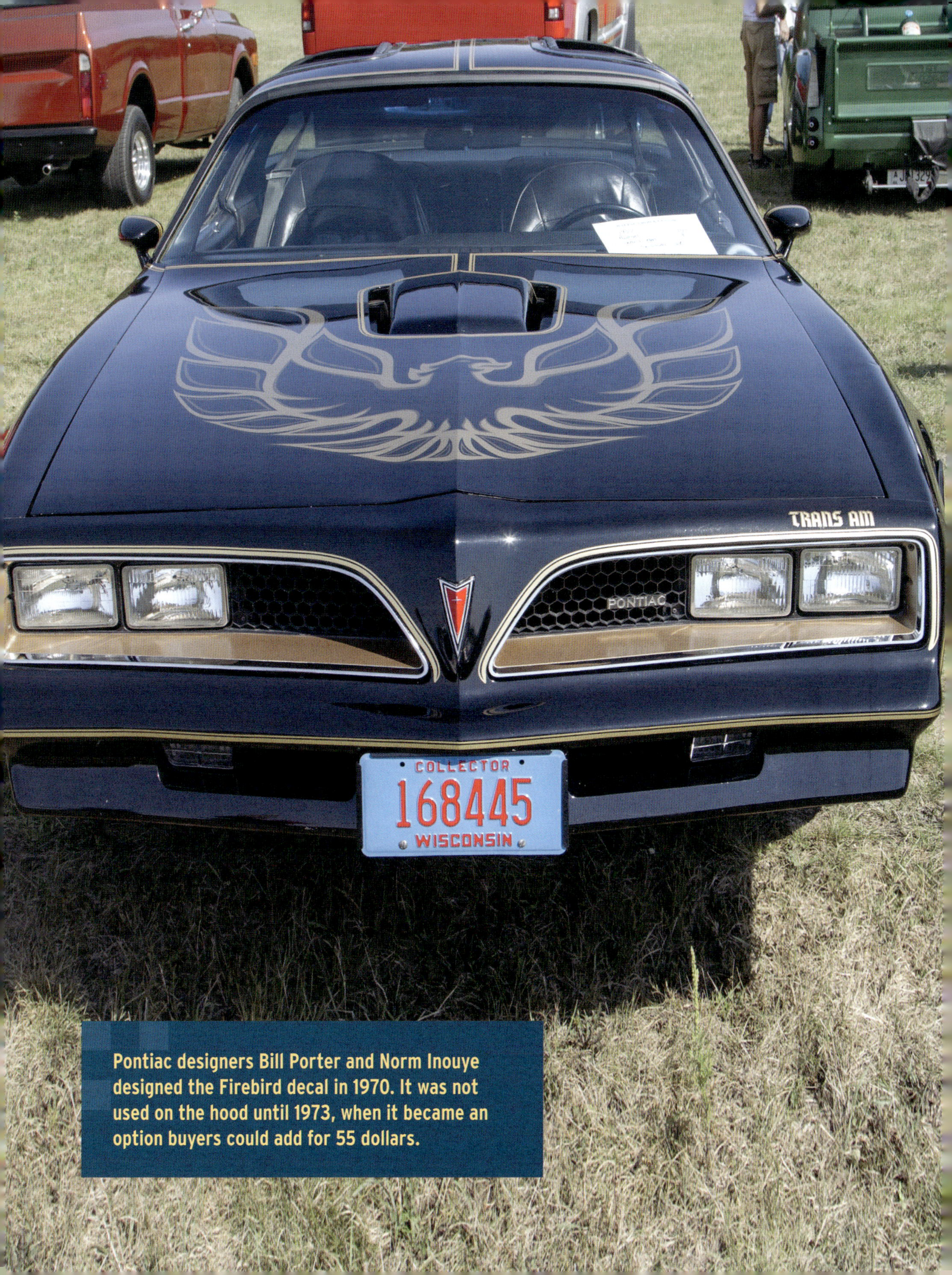

Pontiac designers Bill Porter and Norm Inouye designed the Firebird decal in 1970. It was not used on the hood until 1973, when it became an option buyers could add for 55 dollars.

Technology also helped the revival of muscle cars. New technology in the 1980s such as electronic systems, turbochargers, and advanced engine management controls made it possible to build high-performance cars that also met safety and emissions standards. In fact, this innovation led to improvements in the performance of vehicles from the Muscle Car Era. Carmakers also learned new manufacturing methods to reduce their production costs.

Pony cars saw the biggest revival. In particular, the Ford Mustang, Pontiac Firebird, and Chevrolet Camaro competed throughout the 1980s and 1990s. Among midsize cars, Buick's Grand National and GNX were the main leaders. But most other midsize performance vehicles that came out during that time didn't do as well as their predecessors.

The 2015 Dodge Challenger SRT Hellcat came with two different keys. The black key restricted the engine to 500 horsepower. The red key allowed use of the engine's full 707 horsepower.

A New Golden Age

By the 2010s, car enthusiasts were welcoming what many considered a new golden age of muscle cars. While love for the classic muscle cars of the 1960s and 1970s persisted, new models outdid the classics on almost every front—especially in power. Some models had nearly double the horsepower of those from the Muscle Car Era. For example, Dodge's 2015 Charger Hellcat offered 707 horsepower, compared with the 1969 Charger's 425 horsepower.

Old muscle cars were unreliable, hard to handle, and required a lot of gasoline. But models of the 2010s and 2020s improved in these areas. Their turning and stopping were sharper. They were safer

As of 2023, the 2018 Dodge Challenger SRT Demon is the fastest muscle car ever made. It has a top speed of 211 miles per hour (340 kmh).

and more fuel efficient. Plus, they offered modern luxuries such as air-conditioning and Bluetooth connectivity.

In 2015, performance cars were strong sellers for America's top three car companies. These are Ford, GM (which includes Chevrolet), and Stellantis (which makes Dodge vehicles). And although these new muscle cars weren't cheap, they were very affordable for the power they produced. Other cars that produced the same power as American muscle cars tended to be expensive luxury vehicles.

Sales of these cars have dropped since 2015. However, performance vehicles create brand loyalty and bring people to showrooms. They are a marketing tool for manufacturers' other models. Manufacturers continue to innovate, improving on muscle cars year after year.

The Chevrolet Corvette Z06 was one of the top American performance cars of 2015.

A popular muscle car engine modification was adding a supercharger that extended up through the car's hood.

Chapter 4

CAR CULTURE THEN AND NOW

As America's love for muscle cars grew, the cars made their way into American culture in many different ways. Despite their image of nonconformity, muscle cars have become part of some aspects of mainstream culture. But some people have also built unique subcultures around muscle cars and muscle car hobbies.

Restoration and Nostalgia

Modifying cars has been part of muscle car culture since the dawn of muscle cars. Muscle cars are themselves modified versions of standard car models. During the Muscle Car Era, car parts companies sold parts to make cars faster and flashier. These companies were very successful as muscle cars became popular.

Today, restoring, upgrading, and even collecting old classic muscle cars are common hobbies. No matter how muscle cars change, many enthusiasts are most interested in old classic models. The interest in these hobbies is driven partly by nostalgia. The cars remind older fans of their youth. People can buy the cars they dreamed about having when they were younger. For people of all ages, classic muscle cars are symbols of independence and America. In a way, restoring muscle cars helps people preserve a piece of history.

The Old Town area of Kissimmee, Florida, has held its Saturday Nite Classic Car Show and Cruise every week since 1990.

People also like restoring cars because they can learn a lot from working with the old engines. Older cars are often much simpler to work on because they don't have computer technology in them. Hobbyists can learn how cars work and how car technology has evolved. And many people simply enjoy creating something completely unique that they can be proud of.

LOWRIDERS

Lowriders are cars that have been customized so the bodies sit lower. They are most associated with Mexican American culture, but they are also connected to Black American hip-hop culture. Though many different types of cars can be used for lowriders, muscle cars are a popular choice. Lowriders have historically been wrongly associated with illegal activity. But they are works of art that allow for cultural expression and building community.

Restoring cars can also build community. People interested in muscle cars may join car restoration clubs and help each other on projects. Classic car shows, often called "cruise-ins," are popular American traditions that many people attend, even people who aren't otherwise very interested in cars. The events give enthusiasts ways to show off their work and meet other people who share their interests. Families often attend these events, helping kids and teens learn more about cars, car history, and car restoration.

Miniature Muscle

Muscle cars were hugely popular during the Muscle Car Era. But some people couldn't afford the cars or were too young to buy them. Muscle car fans could instead buy toy cars to play with or model car kits so they could build their favorite muscle cars in miniature. Scale models had been around for a long time, but with new types of plastic being invented starting in the 1950s, the model car industry exploded just as muscle cars were gaining popularity.

Many model car manufacturers were located in Detroit, Michigan, where many major American car manufacturers were also based. In the 1950s, car manufacturers encouraged model companies to develop complete toy models of their cars to help promote their full-size vehicles.

Manufacturers gave these toys away with car purchases, as well as to potential customers. Meanwhile, toy model makers would design scale models of the hottest new types of cars. Eventually, model car companies sold kits so people could build

Hot Wheels is a brand of model cars created by American toy maker Mattel. Although the miniature cars were originally made for children, they became very popular among adult collectors.

their own scale models. One popular type of kit allowed consumers to build the model three different ways: as a standard production car, as a performance or race car, or as a custom version.

The model car kit industry thrived during the Muscle Car Era. Just like real-life muscle car enthusiasts, scale model buyers often preferred kits of American cars over foreign cars. One of the most successful model car kits to hit the shelves was the Monkeemobile. It allowed fans to build a scale model of the customized 1966 Pontiac GTO featured on the TV show *The Monkees*. But, as with muscle cars, the oil crisis affected the industry. The oils used to make plastic were harder to acquire. And the kids who had been the biggest model kit fans were older and less interested in the kits. Some could buy real cars of their own.

American custom car designer Dean Jeffries created the Monkeemobile in 1966. The TV show had two seasons that originally ran from 1966 to 1968.

Today, people continue to build scale models of muscle cars. Many model car companies and toy companies sell kits of classic muscle cars in addition to contemporary car models. Original kits from the Muscle Car Era are now collectibles. In fact, many car enthusiasts start out by building models.

Racing Muscle

In 1949, after the Oldsmobile Rocket 88 was built, it dominated NASCAR. Its success on the racetrack led to increased sales. Car manufacturers realized the effect a race win could have on car sales, leading to the popular car industry saying, "Win on Sunday, sell on Monday." As manufacturers competed for more customers, they used professional racing to show their cars' power. The competition pushed manufacturers to make the best muscle car. Soon, manufacturers produced versions of their muscle cars specifically to compete in

The Daytona 500 is a NASCAR Cup Series race held each February in Daytona Beach, Florida. It's the most popular and important NASCAR race.

races. Some special-edition muscle cars were so powerful that they were eventually banned from NASCAR for having an unfair advantage.

Like fans of muscle cars themselves, fans of professional racing have formed a unique American culture. NASCAR originated in the southeastern United States and is most popular in the South. Many fans see NASCAR as part of American and southern culture and share a sense of patriotism.

Most NASCAR racers and fans are white men. Women and people of color have historically been underrepresented in NASCAR. They have faced sexism and racism from fans and fellow drivers or pit crew members. But NASCAR has been increasing its diversity since 2004 through its Drive for Diversity Program.

Another form of racing associated with muscle cars is street racing. Street racing is very dangerous and generally illegal. In the Muscle Car Era, manufacturers sometimes encouraged these activities to help sell cars and even to test new parts. While people still participate in illegal street racing, some legal versions of street races have started. Often these are designed to help reduce illegal street racing. These events allow everyday people to put their muscle cars to the test for an audience of fellow muscle car fans.

Breaking into the Boys' Club

The worlds of muscle car restoration and racing, as well as other hobbies related to muscle cars, are usually associated with men. Many people assume women don't know much about cars or enjoy driving powerful muscle cars. But women are interested in muscle cars too. Women may appreciate muscle cars for many of the same reasons men do, such as power and performance, nostalgia, and the relationships they can form with other car lovers. Many also appreciate the sense of empowerment and the chance to show another side of their personalities.

Women only make up a small portion of most muscle car communities. They may face sexism, such as people assuming that their cars belong to male relatives or partners. But over the years, women's involvement in muscle car culture has increased. And younger women are a big part of that increase.

Muscle Cars on the Screen

Muscle cars and pony cars have a long history of being featured in movies, TV shows, and video games. Sometimes, they're important parts of the plots or are even characters. The movies and shows help make certain car models popular. The cars also help the movies and shows sell merchandise, such as toy versions of the cars or scale model kits, like for the Monkeemobile. The cars can even become popular icons and symbols.

Many movies and TV programs feature iconic muscle and pony cars. These include classic films such as *Bullitt* and *Smokey and the Bandit*, and the *Transformers* movies and TV shows. Also, many contemporary shows set in the past, such as *Stranger Things*, include muscle cars from the appropriate eras. Video games such as *Need for Speed* and *Gran Turismo* include many models of muscle and pony cars that players can choose to drive.

One particular title played a big role in bringing car culture back to the forefront of Americans' minds. Beginning with the first movie in 2001, the *Fast and Furious* movies have brought powerful American cars into the spotlight. In the films, iconic Dodge, Chevrolet, Ford, and other muscle cars race across the screen. Carmakers saw increased sales of the cars featured in the movies. Dodge has even become a promotional partner for the movies and created movie tie-in ads.

Many people have also noticed a relationship between *Star Wars* films and muscle cars. In particular, a land speeder chase in the movie *Solo* brings to mind classic car movies, and the speeder itself looks like a muscle car. And some car manufacturers have taken inspiration from the *Star Wars* franchise. The 1987 Buick GNX was called "Darth Vader's car" for its similarities in appearance to the Darth Vader character. And Dodge created a collection of promotional Star Wars–themed muscle cars for the release of the 2015 movie *Star Wars: The Force Awakens*.

The 1968 Ford Mustang used in the movie *Bullitt* became a famous pop culture icon. One reason is that *Bullitt* featured one of the best on-screen car chases of all time.

Chevrolet announced that it will discontinue the Camaro after 2024.

Chapter 5

WHAT'S NEXT?

With concerns about the environment, an ever-changing car industry, and new generations developing their own interests, the future of muscle car culture is uncertain. In some ways, it may be on the decline. But there are glimmers of hope and promises of innovation to ensure that muscle cars remain a part of American culture for a long time to come.

Challenges and Change

Muscle cars have changed a great deal since the Muscle Car Era. They're faster, more powerful, and more efficient. They've adapted to new government regulations. But many manufacturers that competed during the Muscle Car Era have closed down. Only a few models of true muscle cars remain in production. Many of the top models with full muscle car options are very expensive, unlike the affordable early muscle cars.

Younger people are also showing less interest in muscle cars overall. Many lack the same levels of nostalgia for the Muscle Car Era that older people who actually lived through the time period have. And there are now more options for transportation, such as ride-sharing and expanded public transit. Today, people often don't need vehicles, especially if they work from home. Additionally, some young people are concerned about protecting the environment and more likely to buy fuel-efficient cars. In spite of this, there are many young people who are passionate about muscle cars, particularly if they grew up around them. So interest isn't dying out completely.

Innovations

In many ways, the world of muscle cars is evolving alongside American culture. One of the biggest changes in the car industry is the popularity of electric cars. Many manufacturers are experimenting with building hybrid or all-electric muscle cars. In 2022, Dodge released a

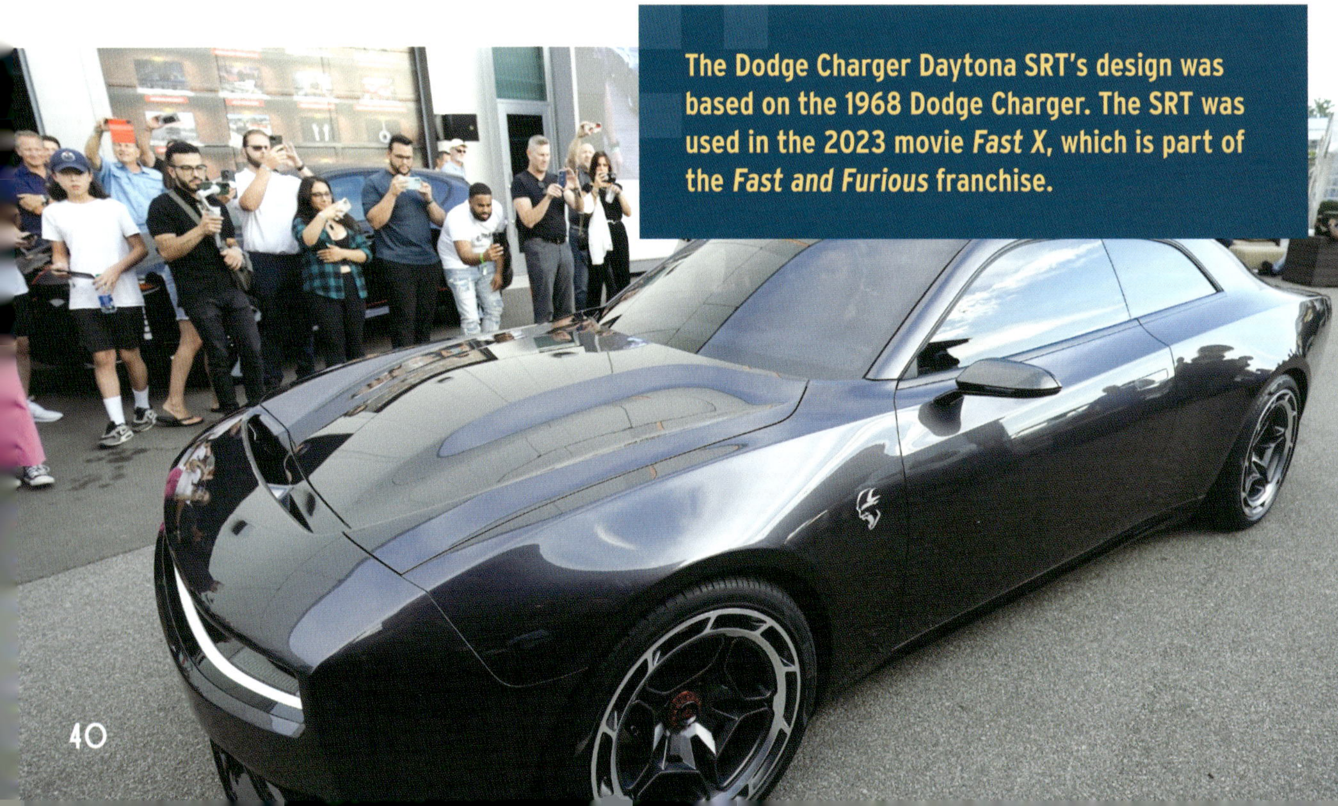

The Dodge Charger Daytona SRT's design was based on the 1968 Dodge Charger. The SRT was used in the 2023 movie *Fast X*, which is part of the *Fast and Furious* franchise.

concept for an electric Dodge Charger Daytona SRT. The company's goal is to make it drive like a standard muscle car. It will even be loud like a traditional muscle car instead of quiet like most electric cars. Other manufacturers have teased electric versions of their pony cars.

Car communities are also expanding to draw in younger fans. Some car shows and communities focus on cars from later eras. The nostalgia is for an era after the Malaise Era rather than before it. Communities and shows for electric vehicle enthusiasts are also popping up.

With their long, uniquely American history, muscle cars will stay an important part of American culture for many years to come. They will always represent a unique era of American history and American car manufacturing. Even as their original fans get older, their nostalgia will remain a powerful draw for many. And with innovations for greater power and lower environmental impacts, younger car enthusiasts will continue to buy American muscle cars.

A GLOBAL REACH

Muscle cars were born in America, and they will always represent American culture. But people in many other countries have taken an interest in them. There are small muscle car scenes in countries including Canada, Sweden, Russia, and Japan. Australia has a strong muscle car following. Racing and long stretches of open roads helped drive Australians' interest in powerful cars. From the time of the Muscle Car Era, both American and Australian manufacturers have built muscle cars for the Australian market.

MAKE AMERICANA!

What can you create that is inspired by muscle cars? Start by thinking about your favorite muscle car makes and models, muscle car communities, and historical themes. Then put your imagination to work!

Design your own muscle car! Get inspired by classic designs or dream up a futuristic new idea.

Start a toy muscle car collection. Use an embroidery hoop and scrap wood to **build a shelf** to display your favorites!

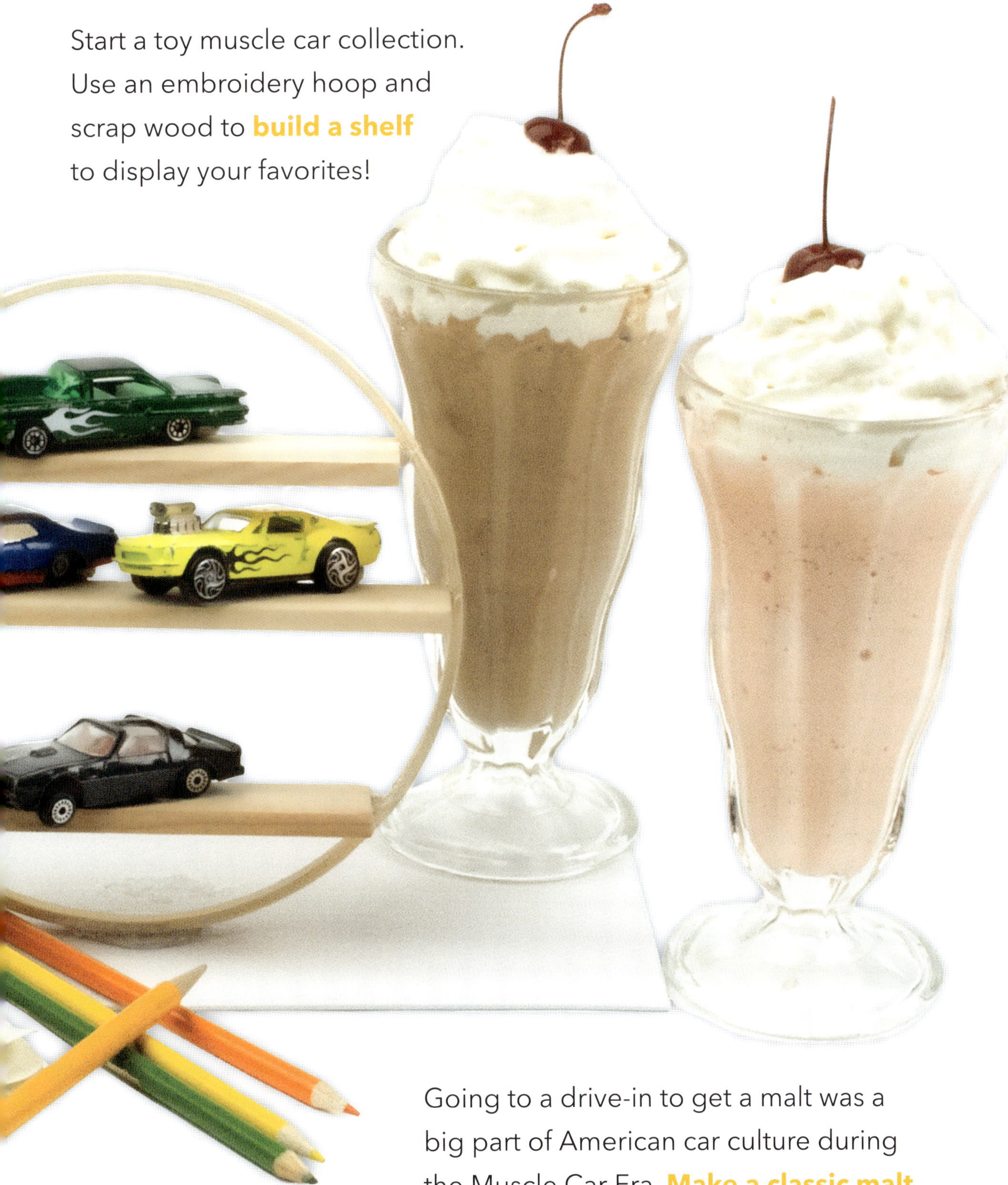

Going to a drive-in to get a malt was a big part of American car culture during the Muscle Car Era. **Make a classic malt**, topped with whipped cream and a cherry.

TIMELINE

1947
NASCAR is conceived.

1949
The Oldsmobile Rocket 88 is released. Many consider it the first muscle car.

1964
The 1964 Pontiac GTO is released. It is the first midsize muscle car, and many consider it the first true muscle car.

1966

The TV show *The Monkees* airs. It features a custom Pontiac GTO called the Monkeemobile, which inspired one of the most successful model car kits ever.

1987

The Buick GNX is released. It is one of the only midsize muscle cars to come out following the Malaise Era.

1973

The United States enters the Malaise Era, which features a gas crisis that further reduces the already low consumer interest in gas-guzzling muscle cars. Another gas crisis will follow in 1979.

2015

Dodge comes out with Hellcat variants for its Charger and Challenger. Both produce 707 horsepower, a number that will increase over time.

2022

Dodge unveils the concept for an all-electric muscle car, the Dodge Charger Daytona SRT.

GLOSSARY

acceleration—how fast a car gains speed.

carbon dioxide—a heavy, colorless gas that is released when people and animals exhale and produced when some fuels are burned.

chassis—the supporting frame of a car or other vehicle.

crisis—a difficult or dangerous situation that needs serious attention.

debate—to discuss or argue about a question or a topic.

diversity—having or including people of different races or cultures.

downforce—a force, created by air flowing over a car, which presses the car to the ground.

drag—the force acting on a vehicle to slow it down as it moves.

franchise—a series of related works, such as movies or video games, that feature the same characters.

fuel efficient—able to travel far using less gasoline.

innovate—to introduce something new or do something in a new way. A new product or method is an innovation.

malaise—a general feeling of sadness, despair, or hopelessness.

nostalgia—comforting or sentimental feelings about the past.

precursor—an earlier or previous version of something.

predecessor—someone or something that came before.

Prohibition—the period from 1920 to 1933 when the United States had a law banning the sale of alcoholic beverages.

public transit—a system for moving people from one place to another using buses and trains.

rebellion—open opposition to authority. Something related to a rebellion is rebellious.

refurbish—to brighten or freshen up.

turbocharger—a device added to a car engine to make it more powerful.

ONLINE RESOURCES

Booklinks
NONFICTION NETWORK
FREE! ONLINE NONFICTION RESOURCES

To learn more about muscle cars, please visit **abdobooklinks.com** or scan this QR code. These links are routinely monitored and updated to provide the most current information available.

INDEX